—THE POWER OF—
VISION

"OPEN MY EYES TO BEHOLD!"

7 Prophetic Things Your Eyes Must Behold

FESTUS ADEYEYE

THE POWER OF VISION

Open My Eyes To Behold!

7 Prophetic Things Your Eyes Must Behold

Copyright © 2015 by **Festus Adeyeye** (Revised Edition)

ISBN: 978-1-944652-04-3

Edited by: Titilola A. Akinyemi

Designed and Printed by:
   Cornerstone Publishing
   Info@thecornerstonepublishers.com
   www.thecornerstonepublishers.com
   516.547.4999

Ordering Information:

To order books and tapes by Pastor Festus Adeyeye, please write to:

   Festus Adeyeye
   Adeyeye Evangelistic Ministries (AEM)
   P.O Box 810
   West Hempstead, NY 11552
   E-mail: aboluade@aol.com
   Website: www.alccwinnershouse.org

CONTENTS

INTRODUCTION

"Open thou mine eyes, that I may behold wondrous things out of thy law." [Psalms 119:18]

"And she went, and sat down over against him a good way off, as it were a bowshot: for she said, LET ME NOT SEE THE DEATH OF THIS CHILD. And she sat over against him and lift up her voice and wept. And God heard the voice of the lad; and the angel of God called to Hagar out of heaven, and said unto her, what aileth thee, Hagar? Fear not; for God hath heard the voice of the lad where he is. Arise, lift up the lad, and hold him in thine hand; for I will make him a great nation. And God opened her eyes, and she saw a well of water; and she went, and filled the bottle with water, and gave the lad drink." [Genesis 21:16-19]

From the scripture above, Hagar's experience clearly demonstrates that just because someone has come to the "end of the road" does not mean that the end has come. When men say there is a casting down, God's children say there is a lifting up. Having been used, sent out, left to wander and die in the wilderness together with her son, Hagar became subdued by the weight of her plight. However, she called unto God that her vision would live. God opened her eyes and she saw a well of water (an oasis) in the middle of the desert. This brought her awaited turn-around. The good news today is that you can experience your so much awaited breakthrough despite all.

There are oases of divine provisions nearer to you than you can imagine. This is not the hour to give up and give in to the nudging voices of failure, discouragement, disappointment or defeat. You have come a long way in the journey of your destiny. God has been so good and faithful in sustaining you. The journey is not over and GOD WANTS YOU AND ME TO FINISH STRONG AND FINISH WELL!

What do you do when the battle becomes intense? Just like Hagar, your eyes must be opened to behold! In the midst of hopelessness, you can behold hope and embrace your awaited victory.

"For there is a hope of a tree, if it be cut down, that it will sprout again, and that the tender branch thereof will not cease. Though the root thereof was old in the earth, and the stock thereof die in the ground; yet through the scent of water it will bud, and bring forth boughs like

a plant."[Job 14:7-9]

Godly and positive change has not eluded your destiny. Job finally beheld good and wondrous things. His restoration became a reality. This is your season of change. It is your season to behold astounding things out of His laws (words). "Through the scent of water..." Water represents the word of God. What you behold is what you become. As you behold the mind-blowing things in God's word, divine transformations will naturally become your portion. However, your transformation is tied to how and what you see.

"That the God of our Lord Jesus Christ, the Father of glory, may give unto you the spirit of wisdom and revelation in the knowledge of him: the eyes of your understanding being enlightened; that ye may know what is the hope of his calling, and what the riches of the glory of his inheritance in the saints." [Ephesians 1:17-18]

The opened eye experience is not about your physical sight. It speaks of the eyes of your understanding. It is the opening of the eyes of your spirit. It also speaks of how you perceive and comprehend things. Miles Hilton Barber, a blind man, once flew a micro-light aircraft over 21 countries using a voice sensor device. As he stated, the most pathetic thing in life is not to be physically blind, but to have your two eyes wide open with 20/20 vision and yet be unable to see. Many are legally blind with impaired physical vision, but are more successful in the journey of life than some who have their 20/20 vision intact. In the words of Madeline Goldstein speaking on the ten famous people who change the world, "blindness is the complete lack of form and light perception. Most people believe that we see with our eyes. The fact is, however, that it is our brain that 'perceives' what we think we see. These famous blind people have changed and shaped the world in many areas such as music, politics, science, arts and sports because they refused to allow their lack of external light perception to satiate or stifle their inner light. The world has been illuminated by their courage and talent." The opened eyes experience thus speaks of the turning on of your inner light so you that you may see "how you need to see," "what you need to see," and "who you need to see." Even though "Blind Bartimaeus" was blind, he had an inner closet vision of his healing. He did not allow the blindness to hold him back from the pursuit of his dream. He saw what the crowd around him could not see and he obtained his miracle.

1

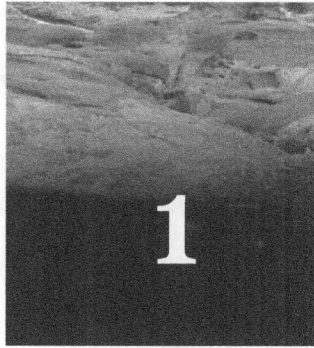

WHY SHOULD YOUR EYES BE OPENED?

WHY SHOULD YOUR EYES BE OPENED?

———◆◆———

1. To Overcome Spiritual Blindness

"But if our gospel be hid, it is hid to them that are lost: In whom the god of this world hath blinded the minds of them which believe not, lest the light of the glorious gospel of Christ, who is the image of God, should shine unto them." [2 Corinthians 4:3-4]

From the testimony of the scripture, Satan, the god of this world has the ability to blindfold people, denying them of the realization of the divine will of God for them. In the scripture above, if Satan could impart blindness on people's mind thereby preventing them from receiving the gift of salvation, he can do so in other affairs of their lives. He can also impede people's mind from grasping and receiving their healing and deliverance and from embracing the best of God for their lives. In one of Kenneth E. Hagin's books, he writes about how Satan blinded the spiritual eyes of his son-in-law, Buddy Harrison for many years. Harrison's life at a particular time exhibited ungodly and unstable characteristics. Although he proclaimed to be born again, he remained a cigarette smoker. He could not hold a job securely for any long period of time and he would quit one job even without securing another. One day while Kenneth Hagin was on a fast, God opened his eyes and gave him a revelation. He saw three monkey-like objects around Buddy; one on the right, one on the left and one in front. Wherever the monkey-like objects commanded him to go, there he went. The Holy Spirit ministered to Kenneth Hagin that those were the demons that had been monitoring and controlling the destiny of his son-in-law, thereby preventing Buddy from making meaningful progress. He was asked to rebuke the objects, which he did. Buddy received his breakthrough of total turn around of his destiny; he became the founder of the popular Harrison Publishing House, authored many books and pastored the Faith Christian Fellowship. Prayers become much more effective when your eyes are opened to the root cause of the situation you are praying about.

2. How You See And What You See Determines Your Future

The future you see with the eye of the spirit is the one you will pursue and embrace. The moment you see the glorious future as ordained of God for your life, it creates a sense of purpose and destiny in you, for accomplishment, and also attracts provisions and resources to you. Spiritual blindness causes people to live their lives without any hope for a glorious future.

"And the Lord said unto Abram, after that Lot was separated from him, Lift up now thine eyes, and look from the place where thou art northwards, and southward, and eastward and westward: For all the land which thou sees, to thee will I give it, and to thy seed for ever." [Genesis 13:14-15]

When God instructed Abram to "look and see," He was not referring to what Abram could see with his physical eyes. Irrespective of how sharp his eyes were at that moment, if whatever Abram saw with his naked eyes at that age of seventy-five was the inheritance to be given him by God, you will agree with me that it would not have been much of an inheritance. Rather, God wanted Abram to envision his future as spoken and ordained by God, with his (Abram's) eyes of understanding; He wanted Abram to look beyond the physical happenings around him to see what heaven had apportioned for him.

Beloved, what you are yet to see exceeds what you have ever seen in your lifetime.

"And the Lord said to Joshua; SEE I have given into your hand Jericho and the king thereof." [Joshua 6:2]

Despite the fact that Jericho City was a fortified fortress, God initiated a supernatural move to deliver it into the hands of Joshua and his people. However, He commanded Joshua to see beyond the fortified, seemingly unbreakable wall to behold the divine hand of God at work in ensuring their victory over Jericho. Joshua saw what God wanted him to see which enabled him to act the way God wanted them to act, and the future of victory became theirs.

3. How You See Also Determines Your Response to the Situations of Life

Because Joshua saw the destruction of the fortified wall of Jericho with his eyes of faith, he chose to walk in obedience and faith as instructed by God.

"And when the servant of the man of God was risen early, and gone forth, behold, an host compassed the city

14

both with horses and chariots. And his servant said unto him, Alas, my master! How shall we do? And he answered, Fear not: for they that be with us are more than they that be with them. And Elisha prayed, and said, LORD, I pray thee, open his eyes, that he may see. And the LORD opened the eyes of the young man; and he saw: and, behold, the mountain was full of horses and chariots of fire round about Elisha." [2 Kings 6:15-17]

What you don't know or cannot see may cause you to panic or magnify the situation confronting you. Fear sometimes is as a result of the wrong perception of situations. Some people have interpreted fear as false evidences that appear real. It is the enemy misinterpreting the situation to make it what it is not. The intention is to cause you to panic and act uncharacteristically. The servant of the man of God thought that the end had come. "Alas, my master! How shall we do," he asked." He became confused and unnerved for the reason of the multitude of enemies that seemed to have surrounded their dwelling. However, when God opened his eyes to see the host of angels that also surrounded their house waiting to help them, his reaction changed; he moved from fear to faith; he moved from apprehension to appreciation. If you could only see with the eye of faith at any given moment, you will agree that the things ordained to work in your favor are more than the opposing force of the enemy confronting you. Instead of complaining and being ungrateful, seeing with the eye of faith will cause you to appreciate the provisions, protection and power of God at work in your life.

The angels of God are delegated daily to protect, preserve, and bring provisions into your life. Daniel fasted and prayed for 21 days and it seemed as though his answers would never come. But God gave him a revelation through Gabriel, one of the chief angels on the dimension of divine support and response to his prayer [Daniel 10:12-14]. Although, it seemed that help was not forthcoming in the physical, God already sent an answer, which the demonic forces of Persia withstood. Despite the demonic delay, God was at work to combat the forces of the enemy in order to execute Daniel's request. Thank God that Daniel persisted in the place of prayer to embrace the divine supplies and support. If you know of what is on the other side of the mountain and if you know how God is orchestrating events to favor your destiny, you will always stand in faith and worship God in thanksgiving while you are waiting for your manifestations. This will cause you to pray in faith, sing in faith, worship in faith, make confessions in faith, dance in faith, give in faith, and also stand expectantly in faith, until the realization of your dreams.

4. Whenever God is Ready to Advance the Destiny of Man, the First Thing He Changes is the Way Man Sees

This was true for Abram; it was true for Elisha and also for Jeremiah.

"Moreover the word of the Lord came unto me, saying, Jeremiah, what did you see? And I said, I see a rod of almond tree." [Jeremiah 1:11]

Almond trees blossom and thrive. In order for the prophetic destiny of Jeremiah to be released, he had to see a blossoming future in agreement with God's plan for him; and because he saw what he was supposed to see, God hastened His word to perform it. The way you see will determine the effectiveness and the efficacy of God's word in your life. If you care to see your future today as ordained by God, it will definitely facilitate the effectual workings of God's word in your life. One of the challenges in fulfilling God's purpose is to know that God has chosen to use you despite your human limitations. Seeing with the eye of the spirit enables you to see what God sees in you for the assignment. It causes you to see beyond your limitation, the unlimited ability of the One who has sent you. It will cause you to dance even in the midst of your present challenges. It will cause you to shout and praise God more than you have ever done in your lifetime.

5. Whenever God Opens the Eye of A Person, it is Expressed as A Vision

There is the eye of the present and there is the eye of the future. Vision is capturing the future in the present. Vision is the ability to see through the eyes of the present. It is your destiny as envisioned from the scriptures. Vision is the inner image of what you must become, as ordained by God; the ability to carve out your prophetic destiny through imagination and mental pictures under the influence of the Holy Spirit. Vision is also foresight with insight; it means beginning a thing with the end in mind. Whatever the mind can conceive and believe, it can also achieve. When you have no vision for life you walk aimlessly, live carelessly, and die shamefully. Get the vision of your life from God, today!

The future you will embrace is the one you have envisioned. It is possible to be in the midst of chaos and calamity and still experience calmness and peace. You may be broke financially and be given a vision for abundance and prosperity. You may have been born in a slum, but vision will cause you not to slumber and die in the slum. You can be raised in the slum and still soar higher than eagles. It all depends on what you see and how you see. People may look at you now and may not value your person; but as the visionary that you are, let them know that you are "under construction!"

On a building construction site, you will encounter all kinds of dirt and debris but once that same building is completed and ready for dedication, people will be invited for a celebration. So it is with a person who is pregnant with God's ordained vision. There is a manifestation of such a vision that will bring joy to the joyless and hope to the hopeless around you. People will soon be invited to celebrate with you for the manifestation of your vision. This is because whatsoever God has caused you to conceive, you will surely deliver.

When vision is removed from any life, living is reduced to mere existence. There is a huge difference between merely existing and truly living. Abram merely existed until the age of seventy-five, when God opened his eyes and gave him a vision of a future beyond his past. At that stage of his life he had no house of his own and he was still living with his father. Everything changed when he took delivery of his heavenly vision. He became the father of many nations and a great patriarch of faith. Despite his age and condition, Abram realized that he could still succeed and make a positive impact on his generation and generations thereafter.

Real life begins with vision. Vision will turn a dwarf into a giant. It will turn the fearful into a bold hearted man. With vision in his hands, Moses turned from a fugitive into a man with audacity. A runaway became a threat to the powerful king Pharaoh. One man with vision is stronger than a   nation especially when the vision is God-given. The reformer John Knox armed with God's vision for Scotland, prayed, "Give me Scotland or I die!" No wonder Mary, Queen of Scots, declared that she was more afraid of the prayers of John Knox than an army of tens of thousands. She knew that a spiritual revolution born out of a visionary is more dangerous than any military or political power. Note that vision is not the same as ambition. While ambition is what a man desires to become in life, vision is what God created him to become. The only meeting point of the two is where the will of a man is lost in the will of God. Vision is higher than ambition. To become truly successful in life, your vision must become your ambition and IT ALL BEGINS WHEN GOD OPENS YOUR EYES!

2

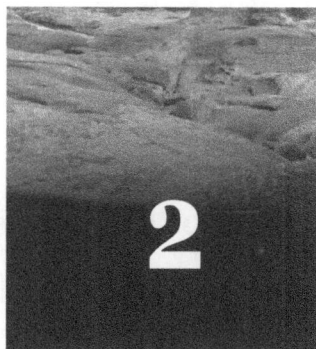

HOW DO I OBTAIN VISION?

How Do I Obtain Vision?

"I will stand upon my watch, and set me upon the tower, and will watch to see what he will say unto me, and what I shall answer when I am reproved." [Habakkuk 2:1]

1. Stand Upon Your Watch

You must separate yourself from the crowd. You are not common, so your vision is not common. Do not look at what your friend is doing and feel that you should do the same. Understand your uniqueness and chart a course as led by the Spirit of God. Caleb and Joshua refused to follow the mindset of other spies and chose to follow God's leading. [Numbers 13:30-31]

2. Watch

Vision can be obtained through prayers [Acts 10:9-16]. Prayers give grace to vision; watching gives alertness and direction to vision. When prayers give birth to vision, watchfulness keeps it from being forgotten.

3. Write the Vision

A vision not written will soon be forgotten. God wrote down His vision for His creation in the bible. Write your own visions down too. If God would write, who are you not to write? There are times God will speak to you in strange and inconvenient places. I have had to pull off the highway many times so that I can write down the revelation received from the spirit of God.

4. Run with the Vision

Activities of your vision must become a daily routine. It should be what you live for. Vision together with action bring about realization.

5. The Timing must be Right

A timeless vision is one that cannot be accomplished [Ecclesiastes 3]. Everything flourishes in its own season. When the timing of a vision is missed, frustration sets in. God's purpose has a timing element for it to be accomplished and so is the vision given to you by God. Since God cannot allow any vision to go unaccomplished, He is ready and willing to bypass any unwilling human vessel for its accomplishment. You must know that you are not the only vessel receiving a vision from God and must be willing to act on the vision at the right time so that God will not pass by you to choose another human vessel.

3

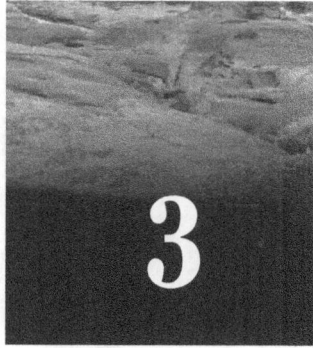

THE BENEFITS OF VISION

THE BENEFITS OF VISION

————◆◆◆————

Since the opened eye experience is expressed as a vision, what are the benefits of vision.

1. God is Committed to Your Vision Only

God is not committed to your tears, but to your vision. It is the vision that you receive from God that commands divine backing. God will do all He can in order to ensure the success of any vision that emanated from Him. So your vision guarantees divine supply and favor. When you are in God's plan, favor naturally comes to you.

> *"Then said the Lord unto me, Thou hast well seen: for I will hasten my word to perform it." [Jeremiah 1:12]*

It is what you see that commits God to perform on your behalf. You commit heaven to work on your behalf if only you can perceive and understand the plan of God for your life. Whatever God orders, He pays for.

2. Vision Gives You Focus in Life

Vision defines your scope and jurisdiction in life. It shows you that you are not everybody and that you can not do everything. You are only assigned to specific duties and assignments. Where there is no definition, there will be deviation. Whenever you see right, your focus is sharp and you will enjoy the blessings of singleness of purpose.

> *"The light of the body is the eye: if therefore thine eye be single, thy whole body shall be full of light."* [Matthew 6:22]

Life is too short for us to experiment with. Vision will give you speed of accomplishment. Wherever there is focus, there will be speed. Vision moves you from the slow lane to the fast lane. Your energy is not dissipated and is undivided.

3. Vision Guarantees Safety

You are safe only within the confines of God's purpose for your life. You are guaranteed safety in whatever you do as long as you operate within the boundaries of God's plan and purpose for your life.

If God instructed you to start a business, even when things are bad, He will back you up. Despite the hatred and the attacks of the Philistines, Isaac prospered and was preserved in the land. Why? Because he was in his set place as ordained by God.

Although God has promised to bless the work of your hands, you must ensure that you only engage in the work He has apportioned for you. Although he promised to give His angels charge over you, make sure that you only jump at God's command and not at the command of self or of the enemy.

4. Vision Gives You Continuous Motivation

Visionaries are self-encouraged and never subjected to shame. In their attempt to fulfill their vision, they may endure jeers and derision, but they are never anxious.

"Looking unto Jesus the author and the finisher of our faith: who for the joy that was set before him endured the cross, despising the shame, and is set down at the right hand of the throne of God." [Hebrews 12:1-3]

In the bid to fulfill the vision of salvation of mankind, under the weight of the cross, Jesus did not express any sense of anger or fear. Rather, He continued his message of love and salvation. He was willing and ready to endure temporary shame, discomfort and pain for eternal rewards of seeing mankind delivered from the oppression of sin and darkness. What is the weight you are under at this moment as a result of your vision? Seeing the future reward will cause you to rejoice as opposed to being in a state of dejection.

4

Vision Pursued Is Vision Possessed!

VISION PURSUED IS VISION POSSESSED!
[Potent Elements Required For the Fulfilment of a Vision]

—◆◆◆—

Visions are very fragile and must be nurtured so they do not die. No one gets to where God wants him or her to be, without a fight! To reach the place where God is calling you to, you must understand that you are in for a battle. You fight not only in order to embrace but also to maintain your blessing. Your victory is certain, with God on your side. A vision is not an idea that you simply possess; it is a conviction that possesses you.

"...Make it plain... that he may run who reads it" [Habakkuk 2:2].

Do not sleep on the vision; run with it! The vision not pursued is one that will perish no matter how real it is. To be delivered, it must be pursued. When one refuses to pursue a vision, you run the risk of someone else receiving and running with it.

1. Vision Must be Pursued with Adequate Planning

Planning your day, week, month and year is essential. God cannot direct you unless you have a plan; however, your plans must conform to God's plan for you. Things do not just happen; you are responsible for making things happen! It is no use waking up daily expecting a change without making some changes of your own. A man plans his ways but the Lord directs his steps [Proverbs 16:9].

According to Ecclesiastes 10:15, "the labor of the fools wearied them, for they do not even know how to go to the city." It is not just enough to know where you are going, it is equally important to know how to get there. Vision is knowing where you are going and having a Holy Spirit directed plan is the roadmap that takes you there. Many do not succeed with their endeavors in life not because of absence of vision but because they failed to map out workable plans. A workable plan enables those who will help you to interpret the vision to run with it.

One of the ways to plan is to learn all you can about

your vision. You must ask yourself the following questions: "Where am I going?" "How do I get to there?" "Who do I need (to meet) to get there?" "What adjustments do I need to make?" The answers to all of the above and many more, will form the basis for your prayers and intercession.

It may be necessary for you to undergo specialized training as part of the learning process. When Nehemiah set out to rebuild the wall of Jerusalem he did his groundwork. After a period of praying in order to secure divine approval and direction, he did a thorough survey of the problem and had the proper understanding of how to solve it [Nehemiah 1-2]. This is known as preparation. It will help you to know what you need, that you do not presently have, affording you the opportunity to equip yourself. No wonder Nehemiah was able to accomplish his task in a record fifty-two days.

2. Nurture Your Dream with Prayer

In the kingdom of God a good business starts with prayer and not only with money. A big vision will require immense prayers.

"For whatever is born of God overcomes the world. And this is the victory that has overcome the world, our

faith" [1 John 5:4].

Vision cannot be fulfilled just by human ability. Only the hand of God can deliver the plans of God.

"...Blessed be the Lord God of Israel, who spoke with His mouth to my father David, and with His hand has fulfilled it..." [1 Kings 8:15].

The prayer of faith is one of the keys to the success of any vision. Prayer was one of the platforms responsible for Nehemiah's success in rebuilding the wall of Jerusalem.

"And it came to pass, when I heard these words, that I sat down and wept, and mourned certain days, and fasted, and prayed before the God of heaven" [Nehemiah 1:4].

The destiny of Jesus Christ was also successfully driven by the engine of prayer. Jesus gave priority to the discipline of prayer throughout his earthly ministry. This is exemplified in the following scriptures; Luke 3:21, Luke 6:12-13, and Mark 6:46-51. As his disciples, we must also follow in his footsteps.

Prayer confers several benefits which include the following:

- Prayer gives birth to vision. Since vision is the

unfolding of God's plan, prayer taps into the mind of God. Prayer also makes you alert in the fulfillment of the vision.

"I will stand upon my watch, and set me upon the tower, and will watch to see what he will say unto me…" *[Habakkuk 2:1].*

• Prayer helps to overcome opposition to your vision. There are opposing forces meant to shut every open door. Prayer shatters every opposing force and terminates everything that has been purposed to shut you down. Nehemiah prayed all through to overcome the obstacles to his vision. Prayer turns your battles and challenges over to God, so that your battles become His battles.

"Nevertheless we made our prayer unto our God, and set a watch against them day and night, because of them" *[Nehemiah 4:9].*

• Prayer gives you strength to pursue your vision. Every vision requires energy, focus and spiritual strength for the pursuit. There are times that you come to a point of discouragement, but prayer helps to reignite your passion and releases divine strength for you to follow through with your aspirations.

"He gives power to the weak, and to those who have no might He increases strength" [Isaiah 40:29].

- Prayer attracts resources to your vision. Prayer opens the divine channel for the release of earthly resources of people, money, materials, good health, favor, etc. Nehemiah did not lack resources for the rebuilding of the wall of Jerusalem because he prayed to the Lord to grant him favor with the King for assistance [Nehemiah 2:4-9].

3. Be Passionate About Your Vision

Since visions are very fragile and must be nurtured so that they are not prematurely terminated, your passion must be constantly refueled. When Satan cannot succeed in terminating someone's vision, his next strategy would be to reduce his/her passion. Passion for the pursuit of a vision fizzles out for many who have become discouraged, most especially when they are not experiencing commensurable, favorable outcomes. The vision that you tenaciously pursue is the vision you will possess.

Nehemiah did not just have a vision to rebuild the wall of Jerusalem; he also had passion for its fulfillment. He continued the pursuit of his dream despite several opposing forces. Passion is the supernatural drive in you to see a mission accomplished, irrespective of the opposition or challenges. As such, the fulfillment of your vision awaits your passion. Passionate people are prepared to put their lives on the line for their vision. Successful people are those who find something to live for and something to die for. Passion is a desire that is stronger than death; it is the stamina that says, "I will go for it!" Jesus was very passionate about his vision [Matthew 16:21]. He knew Jerusalem was a dangerous place but was ready to go there. He came to save mankind and was ready to die for his cause. The pursuit of your vision may involve painful steps but your passion must be stronger than the pain you may endure.

4. Be Willing to be Stretched

Your vision will stretch you! There is a process involved in the fulfillment of your vision. You arrive at the top of a ladder by climbing from the bottom up. It is in God's power to lift you and place you right at the pinnacle, but he wants you to grow. So in the course of overcoming challenges, your brain is tasked to think of new ideas and new strategies, and you grow and develop. In essence, your vision will change you. This is a critical process in the pursuit of any vision and must not be avoided. Whenever anyone circumvents the processes in the achievement of a vision or a goal, it usually results in positional increase without the character to sustain the "new" position.

Whenever you are given a responsibility, it exposes your hidden abilities, abilities you were not even aware of. Joseph as a slave was given the responsibility to run the house of Potiphar and later, the prison. Prior to that time of his life, he had run many errands for his father including delivering food to his brothers. These many responsibilities and experiences all contributed to his success as the second-in-command in Egypt.

In the pursuit of your vision, you must be willing to count the cost. What sacrifices are you willing to make in order to realize your vision? You may have to miss your favorite television shows, forgo unprofitable relationships, or avoid anything else that may be a source of distraction. Abraham had to let go of his nephew Lot before he could properly and exclusively follow God's vision for his life. It is what you are willing to walk away from that determines how far you will go in the pursuit of your vision. Just as Abraham had to forsake tradition and had to leave his kindred, a period or periods of adjustments will be required.

5. Be Willing to Trust God

Can you trust God even when it seems as if you cannot see Him at work? God did not give Abraham too many details. He said, "Just go and as you go I will instruct you." You have to believe God and move forward. For example, at the onset of ALCC, I asked my wife several questions such as "Who will sing?" "Where will the message come from?" Through her counsel and the word of God, my faith was sharpened to believe in the invisible hands of God for provision. I was able to believe and know that God had programmed and ordained helpers of destiny along our paths. As we launched forward, we began to see them appear over time at God's appointed times. You do not have to see the overall picture at the onset of the pursuit of the vision; however you must trust God to fulfill His part as you proceed in the journey. There is no vision without challenges. When challenges come, do not murmur but rather, commence thanksgiving. Look for a reason to thank God. Instead of murmuring and complaining when he lost his throne as a result of persecution by King Saul, David in one of his many compositions of Psalms, thanked God for something that was very important but not immediately obvious as a reason to give thanks:

"I lay down and slept; I awoke for the Lord sustained

me" [Psalms 3:5].

6. Associate With the Right People

The man in John 5:7 said, "I have no man to help me." He was at the same spot for thirty-eight years due to the absence of helpers, but his destiny experienced progress when he encountered Jesus as his Help. You must prayerfully ask God to connect you with "sent" helpers, destiny facilitators and vision expediters. These are people that heaven has prepared and softened their hearts to help you and to be instruments in the solution of your problems, by virtue of their means and/or prior experiences.

Build a good team that can get your vision from origination to accomplishment. Those you choose to associate with can greatly impact your vision. Be around people who may know and have accomplished more than you in the area of your pursuit. Relate with people who will inspire you to rise higher. If you are the smartest one in your group, your group is too small. Be challenged, not intimidated. Have a learner's attitude. You must also have the attitudinal belief that if God did it for them, He can do the same for you. A rapper whose rapping was always on shooting, killing and other antisocial tendencies was asked why that was so. He responded, "That is how life is; that is how the world is." No, that is not how the world is; rather, that is a description of his world as he knows it because of his particular environment. Such occurrences are a reflection of where he lives and what he has seen in life. A few miles away from his environment, life could probably be totally different, with people starting businesses, doing great things and living together in harmony.

Elijah stayed around Elisha and he got a double portion of his anointing. Joshua hung around Moses and he made it into the promised land. Samson hung around compromisers and he missed his destiny. The lesson? Gravitate towards other dreamers. Hang around smart, talented, bright people who are going towards the direction of your vision, and you will get to your purposed goal, faster.

5

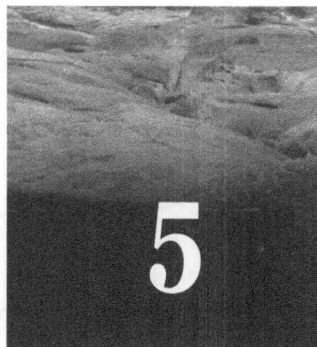

KNOWING AND
OVERCOMING VISION
KILLERS

KNOWING AND OVERCOMING VISION KILLERS

—◆◆—

Even as vision helpers exist, so do vision stealers and vision killers. They manifest as spirits, people, and things that constitute obstacles to the fulfillment of your vision. In the pursuit of your destiny, one of the things you must incorporate into your plan is the biblical plan to overcome opposition. Every worthwhile vision beginning from the Garden of Eden with Adam & Eve, to Noah, Abraham, Moses, Joseph, Esther, Joseph, Nehemiah, and of course, Jesus, has been opposed. If oppositions are handled correctly, the good news is that the vision cannot be terminated. Below are some examples of vision killers.

1. The Adversary

"Stay alert! Watch out for your great enemy, the devil. He prowls around like a roaring lion, looking for someone to devour. Stand firm against him, and be

strong in your faith..." [1 Peter 5:8-9].

You need to walk in the awareness of the fact that you have an unseen enemy whose desire is to stop you from accomplishing your goal. He is like an opponent in a lawsuit. You, of course, are not supposed to walk in fear but with confidence in the word of God and the power of blood of Jesus. Learn to recognize the strategies of the devil and be vigilant so you do not fall prey to his wiles. Satan's strength is in deception through various devices. Learn to be spiritually sensitive and very alert in discerning his schemes, so you do not fall prey to his lies.

> *"Another parable put he forth unto them, saying, 'the kingdom of heaven is likened unto a man which sowed good seed in his field: But while men slept, his enemy came and sowed tares among the wheat, and went his way...He said unto them, 'An enemy hath done this'" [Matthew 13:24-25, 28].*

One of the greatest assets in overcoming vision killers for the fulfillment of your vision is spiritual vigilance. Be aware! Do not give room to the devil. Avoid unnecessary mistakes! You must also learn to rebuke and resist the devil steadfastly, whenever he brings wrong suggestions into your mind [1st Peter 5:9]. This you do through consistent and fervent prayers.

2. Wrong People

People are your greatest asset but can also be your greatest liability. You need destiny helpers, destiny lifters and destiny enablers. However, there are also dangerous and toxic people. Whenever you make up your mind to build your life, Satan can set people to oppose you.

You should be aware of who you receive counsel from, which does not suggest that everyone that does not agree with you over your decisions is an enemy of your progress. However, you should be aware of those whose influence on you is contrary to Godly counsel. When Peter gave Jesus counsel that contradicted God's plan for Him, Jesus rebuked Peter as Satan.

> *"But Peter took him aside and began to reprimand him for saying such things. 'Heaven forbid, Lord,' he said. 'This will never happen to you!' Jesus turned to Peter and said, 'Get away from me, Satan! You are a dangerous trap to me. You are seeing things merely from a human point of view, not from God's'"* [Matthew 16:22-23].

> *"But when Sanballat the Horonite, and Tobiah the servant, the Ammonite, and Geshem the Arabian, heard it, they laughed us to scorn, and despised us, and said, 'What is this thing that ye do? Will ye rebel against*

the king?' Then answered I them, and said unto them, The God of heaven, he will prosper us; therefore we his servants will arise and build: but ye have no portion, nor right, nor memorial, in Jerusalem" [Nehemiah 2:19-20].

Sanballat and Tobiah ridiculed, slandered and tried to discourage Nehemiah and his men [Nehemiah 4:1-3]. It is not impossible that certain people will engage in rumors about you for no just cause other than jealousy and hatred for the right things you do. Nehemiah replied with prayers to God and determination to remain focused on his goal.

The overall desire of the enemy is to distract and dislodge you from your assignment. However, your determination to accomplish your goals and fulfill your destiny must be stronger than enemies' resolve to stop you.

Pray constantly against the attacks of the enemies in your life and also pray that God will send the right people to you. Nehemiah was able to complete the work because he prayed to God constantly against his enemies' plans and also because the good people that were with him outnumbered the bad ones [Nehemiah 3:1-17].

In the pursuit of your vision, you must be careful not to be moved by either the commendation or condemnation of people. You must be very careful of how you handle negative comments from people. Whatever people say about you should not hurt you. Satan reduces passion by bringing negative people who will make negative comments about your life with the intention to discourage you. The number one enemy of a dreamer is a person that does not dream or one who belittles your dream.

You must also be careful about commendations from well-meaning people. Commendations are good as fuel for your passion but they may cause you to settle for the current "best" and not seek future excellence. Do not allow commendations to make you excessively or unreasonably confident, causing you to be complacent and to settle for mediocrity.

3. Self-Sabotaging Behaviors

Apart from Satanic oppositions and the influence of wrong people, you must be aware of any self-sabotaging behavior in your life. Do you possess habits that are inimical to your progress? You must be honest in your self-assessment to identify and subsequently conquer such detrimental habits.

Avoid self-sabotaging behaviors such as laziness, lack of focus, inconsistencies, lack of planning, slothfulness, an unforgiving nature, bitterness, a sinful lifestyle, prayerlessness, etc. Be committed to the pursuit of your vision and never frustrate your destiny through any known weakness of yours. Some people are their own number one enemy when it comes to the achievement of their visions. Take your weaknesses to God in prayer, daily, and be careful not to manifest such weaknesses in your decision-making.

4. Discouragement

Discouragement is a robber of destiny. Discouragement sets in of course, when things do not go as planned. David and his men were known to be men of valor, men of courage and of determination. However, the incident in 1 Samuel 30 affected them so much that they were greatly distressed, discouraged and hopeless. Despite the fact that they lost everything including their wives and children, God's plan for their lives had not changed. Weeping and despair was not the solution either. In verse six, David encouraged himself in the Lord, his God. Instead of crying, he stepped up higher by embracing the deliverance and hope that is in God [1 Samuel 30].

Irrespective of what happens to your vision either as a result of opposition or the normal process of life, learn to wait for it.

"For the vision is yet for an appointed time; But at the end it will speak, and it will not lie. Though it tarries, wait for it; because it will surely come, it will not tarry" [Habakkuk 2:3].

Learn to trust in the God of the vision. Keep your focus on Him and keep doing the right thing. The God of all possibilities will always see you through.

"So let's not get tired of doing what is good. At just the right time we will reap a harvest of blessing if we don't give up [Galatians 6:9].

Those who give up do not go up and there are certain people who give up too soon. They throw in the towel not knowing that they are at the verge of their breakthrough. Never stop fighting for what you want. When you stop fighting for what you want, the things you do not want are what you acquire.

One of the ways to stay in faith is to recall the past victories God has given to you. If He did it once, He will do it again. In 1 Samuel 17, when confronted with Goliath, David recalled how God helped him to kill the bear and the lion with his bare hands. This recollection rekindled his trust in God's ability to help him in his current battle against the giant, Goliath. Instead of focusing on the areas of your life where things are not working at the moment, focus on the faithfulness of God over your life in the past. He is an unchanging God, who is faithful to fulfill His promises over your life.

6

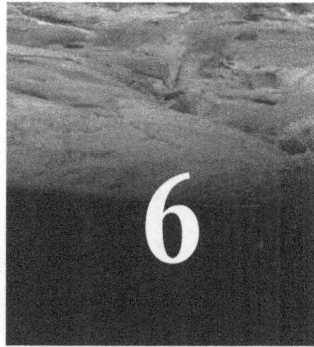

THE 7 PROPHETIC THINGS YOUR EYES MUST BEHOLD

The 7 Prophetic Things Your Eyes Must Behold

1. Behold Your Untapped Treasures

You are not a trash receptacle; rather, you are a reservoir and container of valuable treasures. You need to pray at all times that God should open your eyes to see the deposit He has made inside of you so you can make withdrawals.

> *"But we have this treasure in earthen vessels, that the excellency of the power may be of God, and not of us."*
> *[2 Corinthians 4:7]*

We all came into this world loaded with divine treasures; treasures that are to be tapped and used for the good of mankind and the furtherance of the kingdom of God. You were made for honor and greatness with the potential for incredible impact. However, there is the need for our eyes to open and be cognizant of this important truth in order to maximize our potential and destiny. There must be a hunger and a yearning inside of you to maximize your time and talents on the earth. God has deposited His divine nature into you that can be expressed as divine endowments of talents, gifts and callings.

> *"For the kingdom of heaven is as a man traveling into a far country, who called his own servants, and delivered unto them his goods. And unto one he gave five talents, to another two, and to another one: to every man according to his several ability; and straightway took his journey." [Matthew 25:14-15]*

No one was ever born "empty." Each of us came into this world loaded with virtues and uniquely packaged as a solution to someone's problem. There is something in you that makes you a unique entity and that is your differential factor. Most people are frustrated in life because they always admire traits in others but have never taken time to explore and appreciate their own uniqueness. You must be willing to discover, develop and deploy your unique talents. YOU ARE NEEDED BECAUSE YOU ARE DIFFERENT! If you are not different, you are not needed. Everyone's greatness begins with locating the riches of divine deposit in him or her. It also begins by setting yourself in agreement with God's plan for your life. What do you see at this moment? You are more than what you are right now and you can do more than you are doing at this moment. You must always place a strong demand on your ability and stretch yourself beyond what you have ever done. Don't be afraid to chart a new course. Don't be afraid to delve into new territories you have never explored. Many have an untapped treasure of singing. Many have the untapped treasure of writing. Many have the untapped treasure of leadership. This is your hour to listen to the still small voice of the Holy Spirit. Stop procrastinating; stop being fearful, and start fulfilling the plan of God.

God must also reveal you to you. You must be willing to discover your weaknesses so that you can manage them properly and avoid unnecessary limitations. Everyone has strengths and weaknesses. You are to discover both. However, you need to build on your strength and learn to manage your weaknesses effectively. This may call for a radical change. Isaiah saw the Lord in the year King Uzziah died. King Uzziah was the distraction that kept Isaiah from seeing God accurately and appropriately. When he had an accurate perception of God, he was able to discover his own weakness that could have limited his destiny and ministry [Isaiah 6:1-8]. What is it that stands for King Uzziah in your own life today that may be preventing you from seeing properly, thereby limiting your effectiveness? What is it that can hinder you from becoming a mighty and useful vessel in God's hand? What is it that can prevent the flow of God's presence in your life? This is the time to pray that your eyes of understanding be opened to see these things. Sometimes it is easier to see others as the problem. It is easier to see the specks in the eyes of others while we neglect the planks in our own. God has ordained this season for your lifting and for the fulfillment of your prophetic destiny. Therefore, make a decision to fulfill and not frustrate your destiny. Receive the grace to tap into—and maximize— your latent abilities, in Jesus Name.

PROPHETIC DECLARATION

1. BY THE AUTHORITY IN THE NAME OF JESUS, I PRAY THAT THE LORD WILL OPEN MY EYES OF UNDERSTANDING TODAY AND GRANT UNTO ME THE SPIRIT OF WISDOM, REVELATION KNOWLEDGE AND THE STRATEGIES THAT WILL USHER ME INTO MY NEW DIMENSION AND THAT WILL BRING SUPERNATURAL INCREASE TO MY DESTINY. [Ephesians 1:17-19]

2. HEAVENLY FATHER, I PRAY THAT MY EYES SHOULD BE OPENED TO SEE THE THINGS IN ME THAT MAY HINDER YOUR GLORY IN MY LIFE AND GRANT ME THE GRACE TO DO AWAY WITH THEM IN JESUS NAME. [Isaiah 6:1]

3. OPEN MY EYES TO SEE THE UNTAPPED TREASURE OF YOUR TALENTS, GIFTS AND ABILITIES IN ME SO I CAN MAXIMIZE MY PURPOSE ON THE EARTH.

2. Behold the Plan and Purpose Of God

"For I know the plans I have for you," declares the LORD, "plans to prosper you and not to harm you, plans to give you hope and a future. Then you will call on me and come and pray to me, and I will listen to you. You will seek me and find me when you seek me with all your heart."[Jeremiah 29:11-13]

One of the best things you can behold, comprehend, and embrace, is the plan and the purpose of God for your life. Life is cruel to anyone outside of God's plan. As a matter of fact, anyone outside of God's plan is dangerous. Many lives were jeopardized inside the ship because Jonah—a man outside of God's vision—was sailing with them [Jonah 1:4-5]. No effort should be spared in discovering the plan of God for your life. Your ignorance of your destiny is one of the greatest strengths of the oppressor. If the enemy can keep you ignorant of God's plan, he will continuously oppress and rob you of your earthly entitlements. Saul of Tarsus armed with zeal and ignorance thought he was doing God a big favor by persecuting the early Christians. Unknown to him, he was knocking his head against the chief cornerstone. His life took a new turn on the road to Damascus when he encountered God and he embraced his prophetic destiny. The good news is that you can discover God's plan for your life and

God's plan is good and profitable.

"And I ask the God of our Lord Jesus Christ, the glorious Father, to give you the Spirit, who will make you wise and reveal God to you, so that you will know him. I ask that your minds may be opened to see his light, so that you will know what is THE HOPE TO WHICH HE HAS CALLED YOU, *how rich are the wonderful blessings he promises his people."* [Ephesians 1:17-18 (GNT)]

Apostle Paul prayed ceaselessly for God to open the eyes of the Ephesian Christians in order for them to know the hope to which he called them. There is a calling of God that you must fulfill. Jesus said, "for this cause I was born." This is your hour to step into that to which you have been fashioned. It is because you are needed that you are created. God has uniquely packaged you for an assignment. It is that assignment that differentiates you from others. Do not be afraid to identify and acknowledge your unique differences from others. That may be the key to discovering and deploying your purpose. Do not spend your lifetime endeavoring to fit into the mold that people or society have fashioned for you. Many have lived like mere men, made decisions like mere men, experienced results like mere men and also died like mere men. However, God does not want you to live and die like mere men. You are a walking, talking miracle being. Satan's plan is to batter you while God's plan is to prosper you and give you the expected end. Your victory commences when you discover God's plan and rejects Satan's plan. This is the reason why Satan would cunningly blindfold people, preventing them from understanding God's plan for their lives. Congratulations, as you begin to walk in the realm of revelation and understanding to establish your throne of dominion and breakthrough. You are not meant to be battered and to suffer; you are to reign and prosper.

"What no one saw or heard, what no one ever thought could happen, is the very thing God prepared for those who love him. But it was to us that God made known his secret by means of his Spirit." [1 Corinthians 2:9-10 (GNT)]

There are things that no one has ever seen, heard, or thought of, that are reserved exclusively for those who love God. The latter would be the conduit and the carriers of such things in their generations. The Holy Spirit who is the revealer will unveil them to you. As you continue to fall in love with God and develop intimacy with the person of the Holy Spirit, insightful wisdom that is uncommon to men will be made available to you from now and henceforth. When men say there is a casting down, you will always say there is a lifting because you will see things that make for your lifting.

PROPHETIC DECLARATION

1. BY THE AUTHORITY IN THE NAME OF JESUS AND IN THE WORD OF GOD, I DECLARE BOLDLY THAT GOD WILL RELEASE TOTAL RESTORATION, THE GRACE OF A FINISHER, COURAGE, BOLDNESS, RICHES, HONOR, FAVOR, JOY AND PEACE INTO MY DESTINY TO FULFIL HIS PLAN FOR MY LIFE, IN JESUS NAME.

2. I PRAY THAT WHATSOEVER GOD HAS ORDAINED AND APPORTIONED FOR MY LIFE IN THIS VERY SEASON SHOULD BE MADE MANIFEST IN JESUS NAME.
   [Proverbs 3:27]

3. HEAVENLY FATHER, I THANK YOU FOR INITIATING ACTIVITIES IN THE REALM OF THE SPIRIT TO ARRANGE EVENTS IN THE EARTH REALM FOR THE FULFILMENT OF YOUR PURPOSE IN MY LIFE.

3. Behold Your Prophetic Link

"And it fell on a day, that Elisha passed to Shunem, where there was a great woman; and she constrained him to eat bread. And so it was, that as oft as he passed by, he turned in to eat bread. And she said unto her husband, Behold now, I perceive that this is a holy man of God, which passes by us continually. Let us make a little chamber, I pray thee on the wall and let us set for him a bed, and a table and a stool and a candlestick: and it shall be when he comes to us that he shall stay in there." [2 Kings 4:8-10]

Having perceived Elisha as a man of God, the Shunem woman agreed with her husband to make room for him in their house. The way you see will determine the steps you take. This great woman had a revelation of Prophet Elisha as her prophetic link. She had a revelation that the person passing by her house was not an ordinary man but a prophet of God. This realization and perception prompted her to make provision for him in her house. It would not be incorrect to state that she was not the only resident of that city at that particular time. However, we have no biblical record of others that may have perceived and received Elisha the way and manner she did. Her action caused her to receive multiple breakthroughs. She did what others did not do and she received what others did not receive.

The fact that someone sits under the ministry of a man of God and hears him preach regularly does not mean that he/she "hears" him. It is one thing to be under the ministry of a man of God, it is another thing to be a genuine student of his ministry. You should pray to have the ears to hear and the heart to comprehend the divine utterances proceeding from your man or woman of God.

> *"And though the Lord give you the bread of adversity, and the water of affliction, yet shall not thy teachers be removed into a corner any more, but thine eyes shall see thy teachers. And thine eyes shall hear a word behind thee, saying, this is the way, walk ye in it, when ye turn to the right hand and when ye turn to the left." [Isaiah 30:20-21]*

Seeing your teachers correctly will cause you to be catered for at all seasons. Apart from hearing from the Holy Spirit, God has equally designed your man or woman of God as His voice over your life. The voice of your prophetic vessel will preserve you, protect you, promote you and prosper you.

> *"And it came to pass, that the beggar died, and was carried by the angels into Abraham's bosom,; the rich*

man also died, and was buried; And in hell he lift up his eyes, being in torments, and seeth Abraham afar off, and Lazarus in his bosom. And he cried and said, Father Abraham, have mercy on me, and send Lazarus, that he may dip the tip of his finger in water, and cool my tongue; for I am tormented in this flame. But Abraham said, Son, remember that thou in thy lifetime receivedst thy good things, and likewise Lazarus evil things: but now he is comforted, and thou art tormented. And beside all this, between us and you there is a great gulf fixed: so that they which would pass from hence to you cannot; neither can they pass to us, that would come from thence. Then he said, I pray thee therefore, father, that thou wouldest send him to my father's house: For I have five brethren; that he may testify unto them, lest they also come into this place of torment. Abraham saith unto him, They have Moses and the prophets; let them hear them. And he said, Nay, father Abraham: but if one went unto them from the dead, they will repent. And he said unto him, If they hear not Moses and the prophets, neither will they be persuaded, though one rose from the dead." [Luke 16:22-31]

In verse 29, "Abraham saith unto him, they have Moses and the prophets; let them hear them." The rich man in hell asked Abraham to send a delegate to warn his five brethren on the earth of the terrible condition of hell. But Abraham responded that it was unnecessary to send someone from heaven. Since the rich man's brethren refused to listen to the earthly living prophetic vessels that were with them, they would not listen to anyone sent from heaven. When the voice of Jesus was not valued in His hometown, it brought limitations on their ability to receive from Him. In one of the fasting and prayer exercises with my wife, the spirit of the Lord ministered to us that the food the people under our ministry would eat is in our mouth and that we should always boldly declare His mandate over them.

In order to receive impartation from your prophetic vessels, you need to obey them, value their persons, and value their words. Sow into their lives and serve in their ministry. Avoid any association that will cause you to doubt the validity of his/her ministry. Elisha received the double portion from Elijah because he poured water on his hands and followed him to the end without allowing the sons of the prophets to distract him [2 Kings 3:11]. Gehazi on the other hand failed to take delivery of his glorious future and became leprous because he failed to heed the voice of his prophetic link.

4. Behold A Profitable Future

"Moreover the word of the Lord came unto me,

saying, Jeremiah WHAT SEEST THOU? And I said I SEE A ROD OF AN ALMOND TREE."[Jeremiah 1:11]

"And the Lord said unto Abram, after that Lot was separated from him, lift up now thine eyes, and look from the place where thou art northward, and southward, and eastward, and westward: For ALL THE LAND which THOU SEEST, TO THEE WILL I GIVE IT, and to thy seed for ever." [Genesis 13:14-15]

God is still asking you and me the same question today. What do you see concerning your future? Jeremiah saw a rod of an almond tree that represents blossoming. He saw a blossoming future and God commended him for it. "Then said the Lord unto me. Thou hast well seen: for I will hasten my word to perform it." [Jeremiah 1:11]. Halleluiah! God's word becomes active and alive in your life when you are able to visualize the future God has for you in His word. God also declared to Abram in Genesis 13:14; "ALL THE LAND WHICH THOU SEEST, TO THEE WILL I GIVE." It is the future you can see that you will see. While the last statement may seem grammatically incorrect, it illustrates this great kingdom principle - your vision is your future. It is the future that you see that you will feature in.

"And God brought Abram forth abroad and said, Look now toward heaven and count the stars, if thou be able to number them: and he said unto him, So shall thy seed be." [Genesis 15:5].

This was another of Abram's encounter with God at a time when Abram was in doubt of the validity of God's word in his life. In Genesis 15:2, Abram said, "Lord God, WHAT WILL YOU GIVE ME, SEEING I GO CHILDLESS..." [Genesis 15:2].

Abram was of the opinion that his future was non-existent, but God changed his future by first changing the way he perceived the future from his present. I ask you the same question once again. What do you see concerning your future?

Irrespective of where you are now or whatever is happening in your life at this moment, God has ordained and apportioned your next dimension to be better and greater. "Though thy beginning be small, yet thy latter end should greatly increase." [Job 8:7]. However, what you believe and see is what you become. It is not just enough to believe God for a great and successful present; God must open your eyes to behold and embrace a profitable glorious future. Since you will live in your future, it is better to live in the future you plan.

"A man's belly shall be satisfied with the fruit of mouth; and with the increase of his lips shall he be filled." [Proverbs 18:20]

"For he that will love life, AND SEE GOOD DAYS, let him refrain his tongue from evil, and his lips that they speak no guile." [1 Peter 3:10]

See and speak a blossoming and glorious future! Whatever you do not want from your destiny, eliminate it from your vocabulary and refrain your tongue from evil. Just as God reckoned the negative report of the spies as an evil report (Numbers 13), so also is every word that is contrary to God's word, evil. When you wake up daily, you need to boldly declare a good report over your life. Do not side with the devil with the words of your mouth. You must side with God and His mandate over your life with your words. Declare that this is the day the Lord has made for your rejoicing and gladness. Make a list of the future you plan to live in and start speaking such over your situation. A DUMB FAITH IS A STERILE FAITH AND A SPEAKING FAITH IS A LIVING FAITH. What has your faith been speaking lately? How did Abraham take delivery of the promises of God after seeing it? BY SPEAKING IT FORTH.

"As it is written, I have made thee a father of many

nations, before him whom he believed, EVEN GOD, who quickens the dead, and CALLS THOSE THINGS WHCH BE NOT AS THOUGH THEY WERE." [Romans 4:17]

God's modus operandi is to behold the future He desires by speaking the future from the present. Through faith we understand that the "WORLDS WERE FRAMED BY THE WORD OF GOD, so that the things, which are seen, were not made of things, which do appear." [Hebrews 11:3] The Message Bible translation states: "BY FAITH WE SEE THE WORLD CALLED INTO EXISTENCE BY GOD'S WORD, WHAT WE SEE CREATED BY WHAT WE DON'T SEE." The Contemporary English Version Bible states: "Because of faith, we know that the world was made AT GOD'S COMMAND." The future you desire is in the spiritual realm, which cannot be seen with the naked eyes. However, you can call it into existence by speaking the word of God, which is life and spirit, to bring it into manifestation.

PROPHETIC DECLARATION

1. AS I EMBARK ON THE JOURNEY OF LIFE, I PRAY AGAINST EVERY FORM OF DISTRACTION AND THAT MY DESTINY WILL NOT BE DERAILED IN JESUS NAME. I PRAY THAT MY DESTINY WILL REMAIN ON THE RIGHT PATH THAT GOD HAS ORDAINED FOR ME.

2. I PRAY THAT MY LATTER DAYS AND LATTER YEARS SHALL BE BETTER, BRIGHTER, AND GREATER THAN THE PRESENT, AND THAT EACH SUCCESSIVE DAY AND YEAR SHALL USHER IN GREATER BLESSINGS AND HONOR INTO MY LIFE IN JESUS NAME. [Job 8:7, Proverbs 4:18]

5. Behold Your Covenant Prepared Provisions

I heard the story of a couple in America during the gold rush era, who in search of a better life sold their land and traveled to Europe. They returned to America after several years without any meaningful progress. While they were away struggling in Europe, the person who purchased their land had discovered gold on the same piece of land. The lesson of the story is that the couple lived and sat on top of gold for many years without knowing about it. They embarked on an unnecessary voyage to Europe in search of wealth. Unknown to them, the land they left behind was loaded with enough wealth to sustain a nation. They walked and slept on their provisions for many years without realizing it. May you never lose the good things God has apportioned for you. There are divine allocations for covenant practitioners that will cause them to be provided for, always. Your practice of kingdom covenant principles mandates heaven to make divine allocations for you. Opportunities abound everywhere and all times. Most solutions are usually hidden inside a problem. It takes those whose eyes are opened to see the answers. Divine opportunities usually come disguised as earthly problems. This is the moment you need to pray that God should open your eyes to behold wondrous things out of His laws (God's words). Wondrous things are miraculous things; unusual things that are not common to others but that are uniquely assigned to your destiny.

"Uncover my eyes so that I may see the miraculous things in your teachings." [Psalms 119:18 (GWT)]

There are miraculous things waiting to be discovered, that will add value to your destiny. Irrespective of the mockery your destiny has experienced, there are miracles waiting to be unleashed. You are just one person away from that miracle! You are just one moment away from that miracle! You are just one day away from that miracle! You are just one prayer away from that miracle! And you are just one instruction away from that miracle! God's word is loaded with inexhaustible treasures and provisions for your miracle. May you hear that miraculous instruction today in Jesus Name.

"And She went, and sat down over against him a good way off, as it were a bowshot: for she said, LET ME NOT SEE THE DEATH OF THIS CHILD. And she sat over against him and lift up her voice and wept." [Genesis 21:16]

Hagar's dream and vision of a great future for her

son and herself seemed bleak at this very moment. It is not unlikely that in those days, master Abraham and mother Sarah promised Hagar and her son Ishmael an everlasting dynasty in Abraham's house. They must have appreciated and celebrated her for agreeing to the surrogate contract in order to provide a child for Abraham and Sarah. However, when Abraham and Sarah's long-awaited breakthrough came, Hagar and her son were sent away. At this moment of her life in the rusty, dry dessert, all Hagar could see and hear was the deadly and noisy harrowing winds. All hope seemed lost, but unknown to her, an oasis of divine provision was just a prayer away. Thank God she opened her mouth and cried to the Lord. Never allow any- thing to cause you to shut your mouth from speaking over your dream. Hagar spoke her desire; "LET ME NOT SEE THE DEATH OF THIS CHILD." God responded, and she did not see his death but rather, his triumph, and her son outlived her. You will not only embrace divine provisions to live in your dreams, your dreams will also outlive you in Jesus Name.

"And God heard the voice of the lad; and the angel of God called to Hagar out of heaven, and said unto her, What aileth thee, Hagar? Fear not; for God hath heard the voice of the lad where he is. Arise, lift up the lad, and hold him in thine hand; for I will make him a great nation. And God opened her eyes, and she saw

a well of water; and she went, and filled the bottle with water, and gave the lad drink. [Genesis 21:17-19]

This is one of the reasons why you cannot make decisions like others do; you cannot run around aimlessly like others do. God's blessings are tied to geographical locations; locate your place in the word of God and stay connected to receive your breakthrough.

PROPHETIC DECLARATION

1. BY THE BLOOD OF JESUS, I DECLARE THAT MY MIND IS ALERT. I DECLARE THAT MY SPIRITUAL EYES ARE OPENED TO SEE THE WAY GOD WANTS ME TO SEE. I WIL SEE POSSIBILITES AND OPPORTUNITIES THAT HEAVEN HAS APPORTIONED FOR ME DAILY. I REFUSE TO BOW TO THE FORCES OF EXCUSES AND FAILURE IN JESUS NAME. [Psalms 68:19]

2. HEAVENLY FATHER, I PRAY THAT YOU WILL USHER INTO MY DESTINY DAILY, BENEFITS OF HONOR, FAVOR, PROMOTION AND SUPERNATURAL INCREASE IN JESUS NAME. [Psalms 68:19]

3. I PRAY IN THE NAME OF JESUS, THAT THE ANGELS OF GOD BE RELEASED TO BRING DIVINE DELIVERY OF THE GOOD THINGS APPORTIONED FOR ME IN JESUS NAME.

4. HEAVENLY FATHER, I PRAY THAT FROM TODAY AND HENCEFORTH, I WILL BEGIN

TO ENCOUNTER HELPERS OF DESTINY WHO WILL GO OUT OF THEIR WAY TO USE THEIR RESOURCES, INFLUENCE AND POSITION TO HELP ME SUCCEED IN THE JOURNEY OF LIFE. [1st Samuel 10:3]

5. I REBUKE THE SPIRIT OF WASTE, PROCRASTINATION, LAZINESS, SLOTHFULNESS, SLUMBER AND DULLNESS OF HEART FROM MY LIFE TODAY AND FOREVERMORE IN JESUS NAME. I RECEIVE SOUND MIND FOR MY NEW DIMENSION AND INCREASE IN JESUS NAME.

6. Satan's Plot And Plans Concerning You Will Be Revealed And Uncovered

It is a known fact that the military forces of some nations devote considerable amount of time and billions of dollars to study the strategies of their opposition. The same is equally true in the game of sport. My first son plays football in Malverne High School. According to him, the team usually devotes meaningful time during the preparation for a game to sit together to watch a videotape of the opposition in action. This helps them to understand the strategies of the opponent in order to develop counter strategies. Similarly, in spiritual warfare, one of the major secrets that guarantee uncontested victory is to know the strategy of the opposition. This helps to build a counter-strategy for victory. Walking and living life spiritually blind can result into becoming a cheap victim in the hand of the enemy. However, God does not want that for you. You are ordained to mesmerize the enemy.

"Whenever the king of Aram was fighting against Israel, he asked for advice from his officers about where they were to camp. So the man of God would send a message to the king of Israel, 'Be careful not to go that place. The Arameans are hiding there.' The king of

Israel would send someone to the place that the man of God told him about. Elisha warned them so that they would be on their guard. He did this repeatedly. The king of Aram was very angry about this. He called his officers and asked them. "Won't you tell me who among us is a spy for the king of Israel?" One of the officers answered. "No one. Your majesty. Elisha, the prophet in Israel, tells the king of Israel everything you say even what you say in your bedroom." [2 Kings 6:8-12 GWT]

The Spirit of the Lord is the spirit of revelation. Israel uncovered the evil plots of the Arameans and prevailed against them on all occasions. This was simply because God revealed their evil plans through Prophet Elisha. The King of Aram was very angry seeing that every strategic move he made against Israel did not succeed. At first he thought that there was a traitor in his own army but unknown to him, God through His prophetic link discerned the thought of his heart. The Holy Spirit of God can do for you and me what God did through Prophet Elisha

"Howbeit when he, the Spirit of truth comes, he will guide you into all truth: for he shall not speak of himself: but whatsoever he shall hear, that shall he speak: and he shall show you things to come." [John 16:13]

You may ask the question, why do I need to uncover the plan of the enemy for my life? The mandate of heaven is to frustrate the plans of the enemies over your life. Jesus prevailed on the cross and stripped Satan of his power concerning your destiny. However, enforcing your victory becomes easier when your spiritual eyes are opened, so you that you will not walk into the snares laid by the enemy.

"And Jesus knowing their thoughts said, wherefore think ye evil in your heart?" [Matthew 9:5]

Just like the instance above, there were many occasions where the scribes posed questions to Jesus Christ in an attempt to ensnare Him and get Him into trouble with the authorities. Jesus through the spirit of discernment was able to identify the scribes' wrong motives and He provided appropriate answers to their questions.

Beloved, you have fallen victim and prey enough in the hands of the enemy. You have rashly spoken words that have ensnared you enough. You have walked enough into the trap laid by the enemy. This is the hour that your eyes of understanding must be opened to see how you need to see; to see what you need to see; and to say what you need to say. You will begin to experience the victory you are ordained to experience.

God will reveal all the plans of your enemies to you from now in Jesus Name. This is not an instruction to live your life suspecting people at every turn and making enemies of your friends. Rather, you must walk in the spirit of revelation and Godly counsel. This can only occur when you live a life totally pleasing unto God in all goodliness and purity, living your life in such a manner whereby you saturate yourself with the word of God and in prayer.

PROPHETIC DECLARATION

1. I PRAY THAT ALL THE STRATEGIES, PLANS, SCHEMES AND THE PLOT OF THE WICKED ONES CONCERNING ME BE EXPOSED AND DESTROYED IN JESUS NAME. I COMMAND AND DECREE THAT EVERY WEAPON FORMED AGAINST ME IN ANY REALM OF EXISTENCE, WHETHER IN THE AIR, IN THE SEA, ETC., BE CANCELLED IN JESUS NAME.
[Job 22:28, Isaiah 54:15-17]

2. I PRAY THAT GOD WILL DESTROY AND CONFUSE THE COUNSEL OF ALL MY ENEMIES AND THEIR CONSPIRATORS IN JESUS NAME. I PRAY THAT THEIR COUNSEL WILL NOT PREVAIL AND THEIR HANDS WILL NOT BE ABLE TO CARRY OUT THEIR EVIL ENTERPRISE AGAINST ME IN JESUS NAME.
[2nd Samuel 15:31, Job 5:12]

3. I PRAY THAT MY EYES WILL OPEN THAT I WILL NOT WALK, NOR SIT, NOR STAND IN THE COUNSEL OF THE WICKED AND

THAT I WILL NOT WALK INTO ANY TRAP
LAID BY THE ENEMY IN JESUS NAME.
[Psalms 1:1]

7. Behold your divine deliverance

"And Moses said unto the people, fear ye not, stand still, and see the SALVATION (DELIVERANCE) of the Lord, which he will show to you today: for the Egyptians whom ye have seen today, ye shall see them again no more for ever. The Lord shall fight for you, and ye shall hold your peace." [Exodus 14:13-14]

Vengeance belongs to God. By prophetic insights, this sea- son marks the beginning of the vengeance of God upon all assaults of the enemy in your life. By one action of Jehovah, He ended the 430 years of harassment of the Israelites by the Egyptians. The Israelites burst into singing and they caught a revelation of God as the Man of war.

"The Lord is a man of war: the Lord is his name. Pharaoh's chariots and his host hath he cast into the sea: his chosen captains also are drowned in the Red sea." [Exodus 15:3-4]

Your eyes have beheld enough calamity and adversity. You have been oppressed for too long and this is your season of total deliverance. This is the season to appropriate the finished work of Christ in your life.

"If the Son therefore shall make you free, ye shall be free indeed." [John 8:36]

Many have experienced salvation but not all have experienced liberation. Lazarus was raised from the grave but he was still bound by the grave cloth. Jesus Christ commanded them, "Loose that man and let him go." There are many so-called Christians today who are still bound by the fetters of fear, failure, unbelief, doubt, and all forms of satanic oppression. You must violently take your place in Christ and believe that this is your hour of liberation.

"Shall the prey be taken from the mighty, or the lawful captive delivered? But thus says the Lord, even the captives of the mighty shall be taken away, and the prey of the terrible shall be delivered: for I will contend with him that contends with thee and I will save your children. And I will feed them that oppress thee with own flesh; and they shall be drunk with their own blood, as with sweet wine: and all flesh shall know that I the Lord am thy salvation and thy Redeemer, the mighty one of Jacob." [Isaiah 49:24-26]

Are you a lawful captive of the devil because you have entered into some form of covenant with him knowingly or ignorantly? "But thus says the Lord, EVEN the lawful captives shall be delivered…" Your new covenant of salvation with God through the blood of Jesus has annulled other covenants with the devil. Renounce all forms of satanic or human covenants and confess your covenant with God.

"But now hath he obtained a more excellent ministry, by how much also he is the mediator of a better covenant, which was established upon better promises." [Hebrews 8:6]

The covenant through the blood of Jesus is superior to all other forms of covenants. Plead that covenant and stand firm in the liberty you have in Him. Turn your battles to the Lord and let Him fight on your behalf.

Enforce your deliverance and enhance the way you see through fasting and prayer. As you engage in fasting and prayer coupled with meditation on God's word, the Holy Spirit will illuminate your spirit to comprehend wondrous things. Be a man of the word and a man of the Spirit. Build an insatiable longing in your soul for God's word and fellowship with the Holy Spirit.

"O God, thou art my God; early will I seek thee: my soul thirsteth for thee, my flesh longeth for thee in a dry and thirsty land, where no water is; 2 To see thy power and thy glory, so as I have seen thee in the sanctuary." [Psalms 63:1]

PROPHETIC DECLARATION

1. I PRAY THAT I AM DIVINELY EXEMPTED FROM CALAMITIES, ADVERSITY AND MISFORTUNE. I PRAY THAT THERE SHALL BE NO REASON FOR SORROW OR GRIEF IN MY LIFE AND I SHALL FOREVER REJOICE IN THE GOODNESS OF THE LORD. [Psalms 91:7]

2. I DECLARE TODAY THAT GOD WILL CAUSE ME TO BURST OUT FOR JOY OVER EVERYTHING THAT HAS MADE ME CRY. JEHOVAH SABBOTH IS MY DEFENCE AND MY DEFENDER NOW AND ALWAYS AND HE WILL NOT ALLOW ANYONE TO DO ME EVIL; HE WILL FIGHT FOR ME IN EVERY BATTLE OF LIFE.

3. I PRAY FOR A DIVINE INTERVENTION OVER EVERY SITUATION THAT HAS BEEN DEEMED IMPOSSIBLE IN MY LIFE AND I WILL BEHOLD A BIG TURN-AROUND IN MY FAVOR IN JESUS NAME. [Psalm 126:1-2]

4. I PRAY THAT MY LIFE WILL NOT BE CUT

DOWN IN THE MIDDLE OF THE DAY, BUT THAT I WILL ENJOY LONG LIFE, PROSPERITY AND GOOD HEALTH IN JESUS NAME. [Psalm 91:16, Exodus 23:25]

5. AS GOD DELIVERED THE ISRAELITES BY DIVIDING THE RED SEA INTO TWO, WHATEVER CONSTITUTES HINDERANCES TO MY PROGRESS WILL BE DIVINELY REMOVED IN JESUS NAME. [Exodus 14:5]

6. I BOLDLY DECLARE TODAY THAT THE BATTLES OF MY LIFE ARE THE LORD'S AND MAY GOD ARISE AND TAKE OVER EVERY BATTLE OF MY LIFE AND DESTINY. I PRAY THAT GOD WILL WAGE WAR AGAINST ANYTHING WAGING WAR AGAINST ME IN JESUS NAME.

THE GREATEST PRAYER
OF A LIFETIME

The greatest prayer of a lifetime is to be reconnected back to God in a living relationship. Relationship is the basis for asking. You cannot pray to a God whom you don't know and who does not know you. God wants to be intimate with you. This type of relationship is available to each one of us when we sincerely repent of our sins, and ask God's forgiveness, and receive His Son, Jesus, as our personal Lord and Savior. If you have never surrendered your life to God, or if you have turned away from God and you want to return to Him, now is the time. God is waiting for you. His arms are open wide to receive you. Just pray this simple prayer right now:

O Lord, be merciful to me, a sinner. I realize that I am a sinner. I need a savior and you are my savior. I repent of every sin, every wrongdoing, and I ask for your forgiveness. I receive Jesus Christ, Your only begotten Son, as my Lord and my Savior. I believe that Jesus went to the cross for me and paid the price for my salvation, and now I receive Him into my heart. I declare that I am born again. I am a child of God. Old sins are gone, and I have a brand-new life in Christ in Jesus' name. Amen.

I Would Love To Hear From You!

I would love to hear from you, but even more than that, I would love to pray for you and write back to you. I hope you will let me know what you are believing God for, so we can join together in agreement and turn our faith loose for miracles!

Send your prayer requests to me at:

Festus Adeyeye
Adeyeye Evangelistic Ministries (AEM)
P.O Box 810
West Hempstead, NY 11552
E-mail: aboluade@aol.com
Website: www.alccwinnershouse.org

NOTES

NOTES

NOTES

NOTES

* 9 7 8 1 9 4 4 6 5 2 0 4 3 *